Poems from the Park Bench

Randy Lucas

Parson's Porch Books

Poems from a Park Bench
ISBN: Softcover 978-1-955581-87-5
Copyright © 2022 by Randy Lucas

All rights reserved. No part of this book may be reproduced or transmitted in any form or by any means, electronic or mechanical, including photocopying, recording, or by any information storage and retrieval system, without permission in writing from the publisher.

Parson's Porch Books is an imprint of Parson's Porch & Company (PP&C) in Cleveland, Tennessee. PP&C is an innovative organization which raises money by publishing books of noted authors, representing all genres. Its face and voice is **David Russell Tullock** (dtullock@parsonsporch.com).

Parson's Porch & Company *turns books into bread & milk* by sharing its profits with the poor.

www.parsonsporch.com

Contents_Toc113983592

Introduction	5
Dedication	7
Cover Art	8
The Holy Ordinary	9
Searching for the word of the Lord	10
The Poet	12
I Saw Jesus Today	13
Some of the Best Poems Don't Rhyme	15
Matthew 25	17
A Visit from Things I Can't Control	18
When Words Fail	20
If I Weren't a Pastor	21
The Peddler	24
On that day…	26
Sometimes I'm Mary, Sometimes Judas	28
A Meal at the Monastery	30
The Nets	32
Rest	33
I Walk Among the Fragments	35
Two Views from the cross	37
One Saturday in Autumn	38
Just Sit with me	39
A Friend	41
Somebody's Praying	42
And Then the Wilderness	44
The Park Bench	48
The Fog Once Dark	49
But What If I Knew Your Name?	51
Pilgrimage to the Cross	53
This, I decide!	55
Smile	56
How 'bout You?	57
Ode to the Moment	59
The Things I'll Remember	61
Think with Me	63
The Child	64
The Mirror	66
The Potter's House	67
Live Well Today	68
The Listening Quiet	70

Title	Page
The Quiet Song	71
What a Mother Knows	72
When Death Came	73
The Voyage	75
Struggles	76
Somedays Life Eludes Me	77
Ten Days Left	78
Listening	79
Hello Discouragement	80
The Armor of God *(Ephesians 6:10-20)*	82
The Silence Said	83
The Little Things	84
The Hope I Hold	86
Sometimes I Laugh	87
I Wish	90
A Modest Hope	91
Dear Hope	94
Who Are You?	97
Consider This	99
That Other Road	100
My List of Overlooked Things	102
When Words Become Weapons	104
If I Had One Prayer to Pray	105
The Gift	107
Things I've Learned from Children	109
When You Don't Know What to Do	111
God of the Insignificant	113
A Friend I Found	115
I Stand With You	116
Give Yourself a Break!	118
O Simon Peter, I Understand	120
Accepted	122
The Lesson of the Sea Squirt	124
Ode to My Worry Wart	125
The Visitor	126
I Am Lazarus	129
It Wouldn't Matter Much	131
I Didn't Think I'd Die Today	132

Introduction

Over the years I've collected numerous poems I've written as part of a practice of writing a daily email devotion, *Ruminations and Reflections*. In rummaging through the dusty archives in search of the poems for this collection, I found a fairly common thread. And not surprisingly, the thread revealed something of the theology and heart of the poet that prances inside this pastor's heart.

There are some basic truths to which I dearly cling. I believe God is present in the simplest of things, in life's ordinary moments, people and places. I believe holy ground happens wherever and whenever God make's God's presence known, which means that holy ground abounds! The key for me and for you, is having eyes to see and ears to hear. Though ultimately our ability to catch a glimpse or whiff of heaven is dependent upon God, I do believe the good Lord often provides us with fellow sojourners to help us find our way. That's where poetry comes in.

Poetry often speaks to the heart in ways that prose cannot. I don't understand nor can I explain it. I have no verifiable facts to back up my claim. Poetry can delight and disturb. Carefully chosen words are like pliable clay in the hands of the potter-poet. And though I will carefully stop short of elevating myself to the status of poet, I do affirm that I bring a love of poetry to my pastoral work. Thus, what you now hold in your hands.

Through the years I've envisioned sitting beside God on a park bench. In my imagination, there is no need for words in that moment. I've often reflected that being in the presence of God would be sufficient. No revelation needed. Just sitting with the Divine Presence. Perhaps that's why park benches have sometimes opened my heart more fully to holy encounters. I wrestled with the silence of God while discerning my call to licensed and ordained ministry on park benches. I've studied theology on park benches. I've prayed on park benches. And sometimes while passing by a park bench I've been reminded of my soul's deep yearning to simply sit with God for awhile.

I hope some of these poems have meaning for you. I suspect that even a casual reading will reveal that some came from deeper places, while some were clearly discovered splashing around in more shallow waters. Some are serious, some are playful, hopefully all are hopeful, faithful to God and true to what it means to be human. And I truly hope that you will find something here that will bring a smile to your face, cause to you pause and ponder, and hopefully deepen your curiosity about life and enliven your faith.

Whatever you experience as you travel through these humble pages, please know I'm grateful for the investment of your time and energy. Thank you for joining me in the journey, and for allowing this pilgrim pastor to be your traveling companion for a spell.

Blessings,

Pastor Randy Lucas, MDiv, DMin.
Highlands NC

Dedication

My wife Kathy has been both the recipient, and the inspiration, for many of my poetic attempts through the years. She has been a constant source of encouragement for all my writing ventures, and she continues to stir, support, and give life to my inner poet. She has long encouraged me to gather my poems for a book. With gratitude for all the gentle, loving and relentless nudges she's given, and with much appreciation I dedicate this book to her.

Many others have also encouraged me to gather my poems and put them into book form. For fear of clumsily omitting one single encouraging and valuable voice, I offer a blanket and heartfelt thank you. You know who you are!

Cover Art

I'm grateful to Alabama native and Highlands' artist Jeanie Edwards-Jones for the cover art. After sharing my wife's idea for the cover, Jeanie's creativity did the rest. She is a gifted artist, a vital person of faith, and a really cool human being. I'm honored to have her artwork grace the cover. And, oh yes, Kathy and I have been the recipients of many delectable goodies from Jeanie's kitchen, skillfully delivered to our mailbox by her son Ransom, for which we will always be grateful.

The Holy Ordinary

Beauty abounds
  in earth and sky,
but only seen
  by discerning eye.

In a child's full laugh
  and the aged's sigh,
God's mysterious gift
  comes skipping by.

I've come to believe
  throughout my days,
that God draws near
  in countless ways.

And oft' I've found
  when wisdom stays,
a glimpse of heaven
  in life's thick haze.

And with eyes that see
  and ears that hear,
I've found deep joy
  and humbling cheer.

For in those sacred times
  it has become quite clear,
that ordinary things are how
  God's holiness draws near.

So may we watch with gladness,
   and may we come to know,
how the holy ordinary
   can make our spirits grow.

And if we pay attention,
   life's simple joys may show,
that God is closer than our breath.
   This God who loves us so!

Searching for the word of the Lord

I went seeking recently
  for the word of the Lord.
I wasn't looking for Christian cliches.
You know how I feel about those!

Sometimes I just don't need,
  I'm not in the mood
  for perky platitudes
  or pithy proverbs.

Sometimes I just need to hear
  the word of the Lord,
  spoken out loud,
  or stirring in my soul,
  or confronting my sin.

A word.
A word of truth.
A word of purpose.
A word that sustains
  and strengthens.
A word that convicts,
  shapes
  and prunes.

A word with weight
 and promise
 and power.
A resurrecting word.

The word of the Lord!

So, I gathered all the day's events,
  stuffed them into my back pack
  and off I went.

I had some wounded-ness,
 a bit of disappointment,
 some regret and sadness.
Feeling a bit on the outside

   looking in.
Nose pressed against the glass.
My sense of belonging,
   more partial than full.

What might the Lord say about that?

I don't always find it
   when I go looking for it.
Sometimes the word of the Lord
   is illusive,
    hidden.

Sometimes doing religious things helps.
Sometimes it doesn't.
Sometimes the Bible yields great fruit.
Sometimes the pages seem dry and brittle.

The journey can go on for days.
Looking, searching, listening, praying.
Sometimes my soul cries out -
"Lord, hast thou not a word for me today?"

Silence.

Silence.

And so, tired from my journey,
my exhausting,
fruitless journey.
I removed my backpack
sat down on a hill
and leaned my weary back
against a cross.

And ceased my search.

The Poet

The poet sitting, writes a poem.
   It'd been a day or two.
And hopeful, he sets out to find
   some truth before he's through.

She thinks, now first of virtues,
   love, kindness and the like.
And shuts her eyes, reflecting
   and hungers for what's right.

Recalling now the sacred seeds
   once planted in his soul.
He remembers words, well spoken
   that made his spirit whole.

Remembering now those quiet prayers
   and conversations shared,
the poet thinks of holy times
   with her soul laid bare.

So, what to write? He ponders
   and dabs his quill in ink.
For the poet seeks a deeper thought
   than he often thinks to think.

And then, an inspiration
   as by some unseen word.
"Write of truth" it whispered.
   So clear, as if she'd heard.

For truth, though often buried
   'neath the rubble and the rocks,
in great demand and short supply
   still sets us free, and shocks.

So the poet, with his heart aflame
   now feverishly begins,
for he knows that truth devalued
   is the chiefest sin of sins.

I Saw Jesus Today

I saw Jesus today.
It started with a smile,
and then a nod of understanding,
then a tear of empathy.

I saw Jesus today.
An oasis of kindness
in a desert of cruelty.

A hospitable, outstretched hand
in a hostile world.
I saw Jesus today.

I saw Jesus today.

A friend spoke.
A friend listened.
A friend understood.
A stranger became a friend.
I saw Jesus today.

At the Communion Table,
in the waters of baptism,
in a rest home,
a hospital,
a funeral home,
in prison.
By a sick bed,
with the dying.

I witnessed reconciliation,
I heard a child laugh,
I heard the musings of the aged.
Uncommon kindness,
gentleness,
forgiveness,
patience.

I saw Jesus today.

A revival preacher once told me
that if I welcomed Jesus into my heart
I would see him one day.
And I must've misunderstood.
I thought he meant later, in heaven.

But,
I must've misunderstood.
Because,

I saw Jesus today.

Some of the Best Poems Don't Rhyme

Some of the best poems don't rhyme.
But
there's a rhythm
that's engaging,
at times pulsating.

They waft deep into the soul,
in ways restful,
at times invigorating.

The poet has a language,
the language of metaphor
and simile.
Images
painted on canvas.
A brush dipped into
a well of swirling words.

Different colored words.

For the poet
the pause

……

can be as important

……

as the words.

Lives can be like that.

Some of the best lives don't rhyme,
don't march in perfect formation,
don't align with conventional wisdom
or societal norms
or the expectations of others.

Poems are like people.
People are like poems.

Each one beautiful
in its own sacred way.
Each one with purpose
Each one formed in clay.

See there!
I can make a rhyme!
But sometimes I don't need to,
sometimes I don't want to.

It's OK.
A poem is still a poem.
A person is still a person.

A creation.
A work of art.

So from one poet to another.
Be who you were made to be.
Live, love, sing, pray.
Just be you.
The world sure could use
 a good dose of you, today.

Not feeling perfect?
Not quite in sync?
A bit out of step?

Don't sweat it.

Poems and lives don't always rhyme.

In fact,
some of the best ones don't.

Matthew 25

On Fourth street at the dumpster bin
he quietly sorts and sifts,
wearing a coat that smells of gin
and looks for Christmas gifts.

It's not exactly a Macy's store
or even a JC Penney
but he'll keep searching all the more
though now he can't find any.

A broken glass, a fractured bowl,
he handles all with care.
And on a night to freeze the soul
no one sees him there.

Crinkled wrappers that smell of fish
and last week's chicken bones,
are not the things that we would want
in our holiday homes.

I wonder if they see him,
they that watch on high.
The ones who sang in Bethlehem
whose heralds filled the sky.

For we don't see him, you nor I
as we scurry to the mall.
Though we might just notice if we try,
and might just hear his call.

What was it that Jesus said,
something about goat and sheep.
It's Matthew's gospel, where I read
the words that haunt my sleep.

And makes me think of Christmas gifts
in new and troubling ways.
For I'm yoked to the one who sorts and sifts
in these cold December days.

A Visit from Things I Can't Control

It was a quiet afternoon in Autumn,
  the leaves past turning
  beginning to fall.

The fire in the fireplace crackling,
  bread baking in the oven.
  Coffee on.

Then
A knock at the door.

I recognized the visitor at once.
My old friend,
  make that acquaintance,
"Things I Can't Control."

I didn't want to be rude,
  so, like always,
  I let him in.

And, like always
  he bypassed the pleasantries
  and began running down his list,
  his rather long list,
    like always.

It was a list of grumbles
  and gripes,
a list of swings
  and swipes.

This situation,
  he said with a glee,
is simply as hopeless
  as hopeless can be.

And then, in a litany
  stringing late in the night
he recounted my failings
  to his great delight.

By the time he was finished
  I was so weary and weak,
my mind was in chaos,
  no words left to speak.

And finally finished
  with his fiendish play,
he gathered his bag
and with a nod, skipped away.

And I sat there, like always,
  after one of his visits
thinking why do I watch him
  display his exhibits.

For opening the door to
  the things I can't control
is like a tea spoon of poison
  poured in my cereal bowl.

So I locked the door tight
  and went back to my fire.
And pondered how easy
  to get stuck in the mire.

And I made me a promise
  right there and right then,
  to not be controlled by
things I can't control, again!

When Words Fail

"Words are cheap!"
Isn't that what they say
when words fall so short
of the needs of the day?

Or does it mean that they're hollow
and of small consequence
when speaking about things
that just make no sense?

Or maybe when actions
are what's sorely needed
when even wise words
are so oft seldom heeded?

I just know that sometimes
words just feel so weak,
when our world is so broken
and the future looks bleak.

And our souls cry out
on behalf of the dead
as we weep for the grieving,
sackcloth on our heads.

Dear God! Hear our words
though they may not rise
to the heights of our sorrow
nor the depths of our sighs.

For our best words, you see
don't seem so strong
when measured against
a world rife with wrong.

Please, save us again
from our self-induced hell.
Come Incarnate Word,
heal your land when words fail.

If I Weren't a Pastor

If I weren't a pastor
  I wonder what I'd be?
A poet on a mountaintop?
  An author by the sea?

I could grow my beard
  below my waist,
and look like
   Z.Z. Top.

Or maybe hop
  in my old truck,
and drive and
   never stop.

I could write some songs
  and sing all night
for me and
   the big 'ole moon.

Or maybe sing
  some love songs
to make my
   sweet wife swoon.

(Yes - of course
  she's with me
  in my runaway
  fantasy)

Sometimes its fun
  to play these games,
when I'm tired
  and reeling.

I guess it's helpful
  just to say
you know, here's
  how I'm feeling.

Now I'm OK,
  no need to fret.
I'll be there when
  the bell rings.

Because this work
  I'm called to do,
  though hard, still
    makes my heart sing.

It helps me to remember
  that I am really more,
than academic letters
  or clergy stoles I've wore.

And titles can wear heavy,
  a lesson that I've learned.
Still, what keeps me goin'
  are gifts that can't be earned.

Gifts like grace and goodness,
  like love without condition.
Deeper truths that make me weep
  and quiet my ambition.

So I'll be there when Sunday comes,
  Lord willin', as we say.
And maybe let my beard grow
  some other far-off day.

But if you hear me humming
  some foreign, unknown tune,
I may just be rehearsing
  my audition for the moon.

So hang in there, along with me,
  my weary, worn out friend.
And let's commit to do live a bit
  before we reach life's end.

For we all have weight to carry,
  hard things we'd just soon not.
Still maybe where we are right now

   will prove to be the spot.
The spot where we may come to know
   in new, surprising ways
the lessons of God's crazy grace
   in life's uncertain days.

The Peddler

I happened upon a peddler,
   in a small and quiet town.
His stature, slight. His posture, bent.
   Not one of great renown.

He went about his business
   in unassuming ways.
On street corners and empty lots,
   where he mostly spent his days.

At first I barely noticed him,
   he was easy to ignore.
But I couldn't help but notice
   the town was different than before.

I begin to hear in voices
   of the people I would meet,
softer and more gentle tones,
   words more kind and sweet.

And when finally the difference
   could no longer be denied,
I went and found the peddler,
   at his stand by the roadside.

"What is it that you peddle?"
   I asked after awhile.
With twinkling eyes he raised his head
   and offered a gentle smile.

"I deal in goodness" said the man.
   "Just goodness. Nothing more.
For goodness, I have found is
   what most folks are shopping for."

"So I do my best, to be my best
   to help others be somewhat better.
And I cast seeds of encouragement,
   through call, card, deed or letter."

I thanked him and I walked away
   with much to think and ponder.
And after all these many years
   I still think of him and wonder.

Could I set up a stand today
   and deal in priceless treasure?
For if I'll be my better self,
   I'll be a goodness peddler.

On that day...

I'll see things more clearly.
I'll understand things…finally.
I'll know fully what I doubt today.
I'll get it.
Finally, once and for all,
  I'll get it.
Finally!

Did I say finally?

Forgive my impatience.
But I seek clarity,
  assurance,
  confidence that
  my convictions
  are correct,
  true and
  Christlike.

I'm not sure yet,
  but…

On that day…

  all my errors will be corrected,
  and my theology perfected.

Corrected and perfected,
  that'll be me…

On that day…

But until then,
    until that day.

I'll just keep waiting
  and working
  and praying
  and trying to do my best.

Until I meet the One
 who holds this day,
 and every day…

On that day…

Sometimes I'm Mary, Sometimes Judas

Sometimes I'm Mary,
doting at the feet of Jesus,
enamored by his presence,
returning love for love.
Extravagant in my loving
I'm self-less,
offering pure adoration
and heart-felt praise
to the glory of God,
God alone!

In those moments
I have not one
self-centered thought.
My witness is fruitful
faithful
authentic
true!

But….

Sometimes I'm Judas,
calculating,
conniving,
deceitful,
deceptive,
having the form of religion
not the power.

In those moments
I'm self-absorbed,
self-centered
and self-important.
I keep my sins tucked away,
hidden from view
behind religious sounding words
and religious looking acts,
behind a Sunday smile.

I have a really good Sunday smile!

Sometimes I'm Mary,
the lover,
anointer,
contemplative
care-giver.
With thankful heart
I love with abandon,
without condition!

Sometimes I'm Judas,
the betrayer,
liar,
thief,
coward
and accuser.
A covenant – breaker
and a 30 pieces of silver
backroom deal-maker.

Sometimes I'm Mary.
Sometimes I'm Judas.

But this is what I've found to be true.
Either way,
for the life of me,
I cannot escape
the love of Christ.

A Meal at the Monastery

While lunching at the Abbey yesterday,
    eating food I did not prepare,
    seated at a table I had not wiped clean,
    on plate, bowls and with silverware
    I had not washed,

    I considered the gift
    of being a guest.

    I am spending time
    in the monastery.
    But I am not a monk.
    I am a guest.

    Food and shelter
    warmth, safety and quiet
    all freely given to me.
    A kind and generous
    act of hospitality.
    A gift given
    to the guest.

    From my vantage point
    in the Abbey dining room
    I watched the birds gathering,
    flying, flitting,
    at the red bird feeder
    outside the window.

    Darting, drifting
    one after the other
    sometimes in clumps,
    often dancing in waves
    without a care.

    Without a single
    solitary care.

They ate
they danced
they flew
they laughed
they sang.

Fascinated,
I slowly walked outside.
I quietly stepped toward them.
I had to know their secret.
Why, no worry?
Why, no fear?

"How can you be so carefree?
 How can you be so sure
   what you need
   will daily be provided?"
 I asked.

"The nature of the Creator
   is hospitality,"
 said one.

"And we are
   the Father's guests,"
 said another.

 And off they flew!

The Nets

Maybe it matters little,
which side the nets are dropped.
Perhaps inconsequential
where our lives are plopped.

It seems what matters most
in our living, day to day
is simply listening, hearing
to what Jesus has to say.

And trusting he sees something
that we cannot yet see,
a school of fish approaching,
a victory, 'bout to be.

And following where he leads us,
yearning to know his will,
discerning when to do our work,
when to stop, to rest, be still.

Remember that day when you and I
stood with Simon in the boat?
How the fish filled our nets
while lumps formed in our throats?

And we learned a valuable lesson,
to this day that we hold dear.
We learned all things are possible
whenever the Master draws near.

Rest

Come, child.
Here.
Here beside me.
Sit.
Just sit.
Rest.

You are weary.
I know.
I know.
I feel it.
The heaviness of worry.
The anxious spirit.
The stifling fear.

Come, child.
There is room here,
always room here.
Right here.
Right beside me.

Rest.
Just rest.

There are many yokes,
be careful!
But my yoke…
Take my yoke.
Catch your breath
with my yoke.
Clear your mind
with my yoke.

Rest.
Snuggle.
Nestle with
my Father
and me
and the Spirit.
One.

Come, child.
Be one with us.
Take your rest.
Be whole again.
Here.
Here beside me.

shhhh….
rest.

For now,
just rest.

I Walk Among the Fragments

I walk among the fragments,
  the broken,
  forgotten,
  afraid,
  confused,
  misunderstood,
  downtrodden,
  ostracized and
  marginalized.
  The outcast
  fragments.

At least,
  that's what I like to think.
  That's where
  I like to think I walk.
  That's what
  I like to think I do.

Sometimes I bump up
  against the broken,
  or happen upon
  the frightened,
  or hold a hand
  of the hurting
  or cradle
  a wounded heart.
Sometimes I just
  join in the weeping.

And I think,
  this is the spot,
  this is the moment.
  This,
  this is it!
This is my purpose!

Sometimes I walk among
  the happy, the joyful.
  And I like that.

I really do.
Happy and joyful
people…
well…
they just
make me happy
and joyful too!

But I've learned something
  over the years.
It's a secret.
Shhhhh…
Promise not to tell?
Lean closer,
  and I'll whisper.

Even the happy and joyful
   have fragments.

So, wherever I go
   I try to remember
   my calling,
    my purpose.

I walk among the fragments.

Two Views from the cross

Bookended by two criminals
  on Calvary's desperate hill
the violent sounds of mocking
  were constant, harsh and shrill.

In between the two, an innocent
  was suffering for the lost.
The sweat, the blood, the heartache,
  a portrait of love's cost.

When the bookends looked upon him
  they saw with different eyes.
One only wanted rescue,
  and disappointed, he despised.

The other looked at Jesus
  from a different view.
And even from his painful perch
  all things became brand new.

Two criminals hung beside him
  at The Skull that fateful day,
one bitterly rejected him,
  the other found The Way.

And as the scene unfolded
  I bent my head and knee,
convicted by both sin and love,
  at the foot of Calvary's tree.

One Saturday in Autumn

A grandad and a grandson walk
   with fishing poles in hand,
'til they come to the bank of their fishin' hole,
   a sacred spot of land.

A mom and daughter are having lunch
   two adults, sandwiches and tea.
They both had other options today,
   but there's no place they'd rather be.

A six year old's first college game
   wears the jersey that's just like his dad.
and sings the home team's fight song
   on the best day he's ever had.

And somewhere on a back porch swing
   a couple dangles their feet.
Remembering their lives together,
   sharing stories, sad and sweet.

One Saturday in Autumn
   we all have our own things to do.
Here's hoping you find, in your living,
   memories made just for you.

Just Sit with me

"Just sit with me"
was the simple reply
when I asked what I could do.
I felt so helpless.
I had to do something,

What were the words of wisdom
I could speak to remove the pain?
I really, truly cared,
desperately cared.
I really wanted to help,
to fix things, to connect the dots,
to make sense of it all.
What could I say to bring God near?

Surely there were words
that could chase away
all our doubts and fears,
soft words, wise words,
words of faith and hope,
words of strength and comfort.
There had to be words.
I needed to speak words.
There had to be words!

"No."
"Just sit with me."
That's all he said.
That's what she whispered.

My heart ached.
There had to be more.
I felt so helpless.
I was so afraid.

I searched the bag
where I carry all my best words,
my tried and true,
trusted words.
And it was empty.

There were no words.

There were no words!

And so,
exasperated,
exhausted,
defeated,
and heart broken,
I pulled up a chair.

And my friend smiled.

A Friend

I took a moment with a friend
  not knowing at the time
the value gained by visit's end,
  or of friendship's work, sublime.

We talked of things, oft kept inside
  protected, hidden, quiet.
We mostly laughed, but sometimes cried
  hours deep into the night.

That visit taught me long ago
  a friend's a lifetime treasure.
And in my life I've come to know
  friendship's true, full measure.

And so I walk this restless way
  not seeing journey's end.
But this I've learned, both night and day
  walks better with a friend.

Somebody's Praying

While sporting all the proper wear,
I leapt onto the field.
Prepared with all my armor,
with sharpened blade and shield.

I thrust upon the battlefield
with confidence intact.
While unexpected armies
prepared their sneak attacks.

And quickly I discovered
I was sorely overmatched.
And the battle overwhelmed me,
and all my hopes were dashed.

And the smoke of losing battles
filled my nostrils with despair.
And with every gasping breath
my lungs were filled with putrid air.

The kind of air that fills your soul
and chases away the light.
And leaves you with a breaking heart,
inside an endless night.

How easily the game of life
can take a desperate turn.
And leave us with unsettled minds
and hearts that ache and burn.

And just when I was looking
to raise a defeated hand,
and wave the flag of surrender
because I could no longer stand,

an unexpected cavalry
came suddenly into view.
And somewhere deep inside my heart
I heard a hopeful truth,

that the battlefield, though frightening
and strewn with blood and bone
is not the place my story ends
for I labor, not alone.

For God has oft reminded me
in God's gentle way.
That I can face the battles, as long
as I have friends who pray.

And Then the Wilderness

One day he was baptized,
and a dove descended
and the clouds parted

and

he heard the voice
of his Father,
"You are my Son,
  the Beloved!"

And in that blessed moment
he knew who he was.
An identity shaped
by love,
acceptance,
favor!

But moments pass.

The dove departed
and the clouds closed
and the voice stopped.

And then the wilderness.

And another voice arose.
It was not a voice of love,
acceptance or favor.
This was a voice
in search of a life
to mold,
an identity to shape.

"If"
the voice said,
"you are the of God."
"Prove it!"

And the tests came
in the wilderness.
One after another
they came.

"If you are the Son of God
take these stones,
lust for power,
test God,
come
eat,
bow,
leap!"

"If you are the Son of God."

But,
he would not
eat or
bow or
leap.

Because
that was not
who he was.
That was not
who he was.

And you,
child of God,
beloved,
accepted,
favored,

you've known the
rich blessings
of faith
and trust,
of family
and friends,

you have known
the exquisite joy

of being loved,
valued and
cherished.

You've been
confidant
in your identity.
You're faith
has been strong.

And then the wilderness.

And the voice
in the wilderness
whispers to you,
too

calling into question
that you are
beloved,
accepted,
favored.

And the voice
in the wilderness
can be convincing.
It's had practice.

It will try to make
you forget
your identity.
It will try to
shape you,
and mold you
into something
or someone
you are not.

Don't listen!

Today,
I've been sent to you,
especially to you,

specifically for you
child of God,
beloved,
accepted,
favored.

Simply to remind you
who you are!

The Park Bench

How 'oft I've spent my waking hours
  in pursuits heroic, grand.
In search of deeper meanings,
  reaching for a guiding hand.

But somewhere back along the way
  a quieter wisdom dawned.
And I began a humbler quest,
  bidding grander goals, "so long."

The spiritual life, I've come to see
  is not won by leap or bound.
But in many quiet, hidden ways,
  feet planted on the ground.

So I think of God on a park bench,
  laying aside all thoughts, profound.
And drawing near, invited,
  I walk over and sit down.

The Fog Once Dark

One day the way was hard to see,
    no matter how I tried.
And so in prayer I sought relief,
    and to the Lord, I cried.

"Oh God," my soul cried out in pain.
    It was an honest plea.
"Hast thou not kept, a blessing near
    that thou couldst lend to me?"

The desperate cries, continued thus
    until my soul grew faint.
And weary grew the inner groan
    that bore the heavy weight.

And just when hope had packed her bags
    and headed for the door
I then remembered something
    I had learned some years before.

The echoes of that distant truth
    from somewhere deep inside,
were whispers first, then shouting
    that the darkness could not hide.

And hope? She put her bags away
    pulled up a chair, and smiled.
And we talked about the truth
    I hadn't thought of in awhile.

The truth that fog had shadowed,
    as it cluttered dark my mind.
The truth of love and beauty,
    wisdom pure, and grace divine.

The truth that God is nearer
    than the way I sought to see.
The truth of God surrounding,
    the truth of God, in me.

And suddenly life's fragments
   took on the air of gift.
And hope and me, refilled our cups
   as the fog began to lift.

But What If I Knew Your Name?

You look so different from me,
  the color of your skin
  the sound of your voice.
  Your culture.
  Your language.
  You're one of them,
   those people.
  You're different from me.
  Different people make me nervous.
  I don't really trust different.

But what if I knew your name?

  There's a label for you.
  Were you born with it,
  or did society give it to you?
  You're a category,
  a statistic.
  I don't think I can trust you.
  Nothing personal.

But what if I knew your name?

  Your desires, they're just -
  they're just unnatural.
  Unholy.
  Unclean.
  You're unclean.
  Isn't that what the Bible says?
  I'm sure that's what it means,
  isn't it?
  Its not that I'm judgmental.
  Its just…
  I don't know.
  I just don't get it.
  I can't understand you.
  I really don't trust different.

But what if I knew your name?

Maybe it'd be different
  if all labels fell away.
And if I listened longer
  before considering what to say.

Maybe then I'd come to know
  what it is that makes you, you.
And maybe then, I'd bless the Lord,
  a bit more before I'm through.

So maybe I should remember
  that life is not a game.
And then, perhaps begin again.
  Please tell me, what is your name?

Pilgrimage to the Cross

I saw a cross, so far away
  beyond the distant range.
Drawn, I made my journey thus.
  It's beckon, stark and strange.

Perhaps I went for answers,
  though reasoning was unclear.
I only knew I dared not stop,
  it's calling drew me near.

I passed by fellow travelers,
  reveling without a care.
"Mere foolishness!" they mocked me,
  as they laughed, teased and stared.

At times I almost turned around,
  to join them in their glee.
For even though I journeyed on,
  rewards, I could not see.

The cross on the horizon,
  grew larger in my view,
and I began to see the signs
  of suffering, someone knew.

Then I began to think again,
  of wounds I've known in life,
of fears, regrets and failures,
  of conflict, grief and strife.

And as I walked I wondered
  from somewhere deep inside.
What was the cross's meaning?
  Who was the One who died?

And then another traveler
  there on the road that day,
nodding said, "You're welcome."
  smiled, winked, and walked away.

I noticed scars upon his hands,
   but didn't ask him why.
Then from somewhere deep inside,
   "Are you the One?" I cried.

And then I saw, my journey
   had brought me to the cross,
and everything I ever gained,
   seemed nothing now, but loss.

And my fears? I couldn't find them,
   standing at the cross that day.
And wiping one tear, then another,
   I bowed my head and prayed.

This, I decide!

I make this declaration!
My promise to the universe.
I will not add to life's sorrows.
I will not make matters worse!

This, I decide!

I will not speak harmful words.
I will not turn a deaf ear,
  but I will listen to the other.
I reject ignorance, hatred and fear.

This, I decide!

I will not spread gossip.
I will not contribute to the divide.
I will not engage in cruelty.
This, I hereby decide!

I will seek understanding,
I will chose tolerance and grace.
I will stand with the outcast,
  and see Jesus' face.

This, I decide!

There are things beyond me,
  I'm powerless to change.
But something stirs within me,
  something powerful, and strange.

It drives me to a deep place,
  where I see and understand.
That God can help us change things.
So, come friend. Take my hand.

Smile

Life, with all her frailties,
imperfect hidden subtleties,
is difficult to say the least,
charging like an untamed beast.

And here I sit, with hat in hand,
trying hard to understand,
with limited ability,
beyond my capability.

I can't, no matter how I try,
plant both my feet and touch the sky.
And when frustrations seem to mount,
with struggle's toll's too much to count.

I catch a glimpse of something fair,
eternal, as if always there,
that makes my journey seem worthwhile,
a simple beauty called a smile.

And as I shake despair's thick dust,
insecurities give way to trust.
And as my spirit starts to lift,
I'm reminded how a smile's a gift.

So friend, please hear me as I say,
that someone who you'll meet today,
is desperate for a friendly smile,
because, for some, it's been awhile.

And maybe, if the good Lord wills,
your smile today will cure some ills
for someone, up against life's rope
who'll find your smile a sign of hope.

So don't dare think you don't possess,
the ability to lighten stress.
For with one smile from you today,
you may help us all, to find our way.

How 'bout You?

A man I saw on the corner one day
 with tattered shirt and sweater.
I didn't want to look at him,
 because I just knew better.

For I'd seen his like at other times,
 messaged cardboard in hand.
Standing at the off ramp,
 a blight upon our land.

And though I'm not the judging type,
 at least not in my mind.
For I was raised to be polite,
 compassionate and kind.

And though I did not try to look
 in the eyes of the man that day.
I couldn't help but see his face
 when he quietly looked my way.

"Don't be afraid," he assured me,
 and gave a knowing smile.
I'm not going to ask for money,
 that's really not my style.

"But I would like for you to see me
 as you quickly pass me by.
For a man sometimes feels like a ghost,
 when no one looks him in the eye.

"And though my life is hard at times,
 I'm still grateful for each day.
And I hope the good Lord blesses you."
 Then he waved, and walked away.

And I stood there, lost inside my head
 and thought about his word,
that somehow pierced my hardened heart,
 like some new truth just heard.

I wondered about the other folks
  who I've treated like a ghost.
The ones ignored like cattle
  who needed a smile the most.

So I carry now inside my heart
  his lesson, timeless and true.
Everyone needs to know they matter.
  I get that now. How 'bout you?

Ode to the Moment

Life. Moves. Fast.
  Very fast.
  So fast.
  Too fast.
Here now.
Then gone!

"Wow!
Did you see it?"
  "What?"
"The moment!

 Never mind…
 Its gone."

A moment's life span
  is, well
  momentary.
Here one moment.
Gone the next.

When today's moments
  become yesterday's moments,
  then we get it.
  We finally get it.
  The value of moments
  is clearer in the rearview mirror.

Why is that?

Why do we miss so many moments?
Why are moments valued most
  in our memories?

I don't know.
I'm sorry,
  I don't have the answer.

But maybe, just for today
  you and I
  can try.
Maybe we can try
  something different.

Maybe for today
  we can
  dismiss the distractions,
  nullify the noise,
  reject the regrets,
  send away the shame,
and live as one
  unfettered by failures,
  not yoked to yesterday.

And honor the day.
And cherish the moment.
And live.

Live, my sister!
Live, my brother!
Honoring,
cherishing,
embracing

the beautiful
fleeting,
valuable,
moment.

The Things I'll Remember

The things I'll remember
　when my day is done
won't be all the victories,
　or hard battles won.

But rather, I think
　my focus will be
on simple reminders
　of good things to see.

I'll think of the times, when
　a gentle word spoken
brought me some healing
　when my heart was broken.

I believe I'll recall
　when a friend really heard
the cares of my heart,
　holding sacred each word.

When night closes in
　and I fade into memory,
I'll be grateful for life,
　its beauty and symmetry.

And regretting those things
　I too quickly passed by,
I'll long for more time,
　for just one more try.

But of course that's just not
　the way things can be.
So I better look now
　at the things I can see.

And love while I can
　and sing in the rain,
and try to relieve
　somebody's real pain.

For life is a gift
  isn't that what they say?
So, let's you and I live
  like we mean it today!

Whaddaya say?

Think with Me

Think with me for just a bit
  on the things you'll do today.
Let's talk about the walk you'll walk
  and about the words you'll say.

Let's ponder how the day will go
  for those who cross your path.
Will their loads be lightened just a bit
  or perhaps endure your wrath?

Will kindness be a virtue
  displayed for all to see?
Or will the focus of your day
  be me, and me, and me?

Could a friend easily find a friend
  and a needy stranger too,
who'd help them navigate the day?
  Might such a friend be you?

For Mondays can be hard for some,
  like any day of the week.
And journeys can be filled with days
  that are rainy, dark and bleak.

So think with me before you leave
  and venture out the door.
And consider, you may have the grace
  the world is desperate for.

So love, forgive, welcome, smile
  and live as one who knows
that hope is found in every life
  where goodness lives and grows.

And if you will allow me
  this hunch before I'm through.
This day someone will soon be blessed
  by the gift of Christ in you!

The Child

The frightened child with downward gaze
   and trembling lips fast stayed.
Without a whimper or a sound
   uncertain and afraid.

The night was dark like none before
   as fearful dread drew near.
And the child withdrew in quiet hope
   to hide from crippling fear.

Outside the world was bustling fast
   with sirens loud and racing,
and this moment seemed so far away.
What was the cold world facing?

Distant voices now were heard
   above the hidden deep.
As if the child was waking now
   from a deeper, darker sleep.

Then a Presence seemed to fill the void,
   dark yielding to the light.
And with calmness like no calm before
   came a dawn to end the night.

And then the fear subsided
   in the clarity of a thought.
For childhood's days were miles away
   as life's last thread stretched taut.

And the worry that had gripped this child,
   from childhood long removed,
was not so much like worry now,
   but more like hope, renewed.

And trust, much like a cotton sheet
   pulled gently o'er the face
along with comfort, peace and love
   expelled fear's final trace.

And though the years were many
 from birth until this day.
That first moment in the Savior's arms
 was like a giddy child at play.

The Mirror

A difficult day sent me searching to find
  the source of most of my trials.
And so I began a desperate search.
  It covered quite a few miles.

I suspected first, my neighbor
  who sometimes gives me grief.
And I thought if I could prove his guilt
  it would be a grand relief.

Or maybe perhaps the teller
  at my bank who can't seem to smile.
I was determined to find the culprit,
  even though it could take a while.

Or maybe the kid at the drive thru
  who never remembers my fries.
Or the politician I've seen on tv
  whose forever, it seems, tellin' lies.

It could be my spouse, now that's a thought
  worthy of thinking again.
For finding fault's OK, right?
  Surely blaming's not really a sin.

But in a breath of clarity
  before darting out to work.
I thought of all the people I'd blamed
  and suddenly felt like a jerk.

For standing in front of the mirror
  that day I could finally see,
the person who most needed changing
  was in the mirror, facing me.

Live Well Today

Dear Friend,

   I want you to live well today.

   I'm not so concerned with what you have,
     or what you will receive.
This isn't about stuff,
     or accolades,
     not about material things,
     or acquisition, accumulation
     or accomplishments.

   I want you to live well today.

   I want you to prosper in spirit,
     increase in virtue,
     expand and multiply
     your capability for goodness.

   I want you to speak with wisdom,
     listen with compassion,
     serve with joy,
     love at great risk.

   I want you to live well today.

   And I want you to know something,
     something very important.
Lean close.
Closer.
I want you know that you matter,
     that your life,
     your work,
     your words,
     your witness
     is not inconsequential.

   That goes for your neighbor too.
   You know the one I'm talking about.

The Potter's House

Sometimes I'm like a blob of clay,
spinning on the potter's wheel.
Misshapen, twisted, hopeless,
at least that's how I feel.

Trying hard to do my best,
but everything goes for naught.
"How to make a mess of things,"
is a course I could have taught.

Yet something stirs inside me.
And I somehow do believe,
that even messy blobs sometimes
can hope for a reprieve.

For I know a patient Potter,
who gently molds the clay,
who delights in making all things new
each and every day.

And even clay that's weary
and hardened by lost hope,
like blistered hands that struggle,
at the end of a frayed rope,

is soft and moist and pliable
cradled in the Master's hands,
and shaped and formed and molded
into something new and grand.

So just in case your feeling
like a big ole lump of clay,
let's go down to the potter's house.
Come, I'll show you the way.

And I want you to know
  you have purpose,
  and value,
  and that you are unique,
  and that, at some point
  the rest of us will need you to do
  what only you can do.

Be uniquely you.

And that means being fully
   who you have been created to be,
   living into the fullness of God's intent for you,
   letting the world catch a glimpse
   of the image of God in you.

So live today
   as one who understands
   that life's greatest purpose
   is to glorify the One
   who gives us life.

I want you to live well today,
   to the glory of God

The Listening Quiet

There's a moment that lives
　in the vast sea of words,
that's often ignored,
　　and too seldom heard.

At the crosshairs of thought
　and strong held beliefs,
sitting quiet with all
　who seek conflict's relief.

A pause, nothing more,
　a breath taken and held.
A pivoting moment.
　　Impatience expelled.

Listen, can you hear it
　rising up from within,
that quiet before
　understanding begins?

We let our mouths rest
　and open our ears,
and listen to others,
　unfettered by fears.

For sometimes it's better
　to hear than be heard.
For listening, you see
　　is a much needed word.

The Quiet Song

Imperceptible to the ear,
   it's melody in hiding.
A sound of silence resting
   deep within the heart abiding.

The evidence of many wounds,
   stirred melodies unbidden.
Far beneath the world's keen eye,
   lies beauty deep, and hidden.

For a quiet song is breathing,
   and with each breath it brings,
a hope that's born of mystery
   and sounds of angel's wings.

And though the world may miss it
   as it rises in the soul,
the one who sings in silence,
   sings a song to make us whole.

So sing, beloved child of God
   though the world may never hear.
Sing silently your songs of praise
   to the Spirit who draws near.

And walk in clear assurance
   through this world of right and wrong.
For soon we all may hum the tune
   of your hope-filled, quiet song.

What a Mother Knows

There are many grand things of deep, great import,
   you can't count on your fingers and toes.
Like quiet held hurts and comforted fears,
   things that a mother's heart knows.

There are playful joys in childhood years,
   like playing outside when it snows.
And homemade treats to warm the heart,
   those little, huge, things that mom knows.

And when your heart breaks, her heart breaks too,
   alongside you through highs and the lows.
For when her child's hurting, she feels the pain.
   The cost of love she deeply knows.

But what of the mothers, who, broken themselves
   perpetuate deep wounds and woes?
For childhood trauma that lingers for years,
   is a pain the hurt grown-up child knows.

So we pray for the hurting, and give praise where its due,
   grateful for the fruit that love shows.
And pray to the Lord, with a deep longing hope -
   one day love is what every child knows.

When Death Came

Death came calling,
  unexpectedly.
I wasn't ready.
I told Death so.

"I'm not ready!"

"Not now.
There's so much to do.
So much I haven't done.
So much I've planned to do.

"I'm not ready!"

"Okay,"
said Death.
And went away.

And I got busy for awhile.
But it didn't last long.
Soon I forgot.
The urgency was gone.

Then one day
Death returned.

"I gave you extra time,"
said Death.
"Now your time is up."

"No! No!
I protested.
It can't possibly be today!

"I have cards to write
and visits to make,
and encouragement I've been
  really meaning to offer,
and many acts of kindness
  and love and mercy

I've really been thinking
a lot about lately.

"Really!"

"Okay"
said Death.
And went away.
Then the alarm went off!

I bolted up in bed
wiped my eyes
and shook the
  sleepy cobwebs
  from my head.

"It was a dream"
I said.
"Just a dream."

I was glad.

Then I walked into my study,
  took down a box of cards from the shelf
  sat down,
  and started to write!

The Voyage

The maiden voyage of kindly acts
  dispersed dockside and sailed,
and gallantly to sea set forth.
  Her beauty, we beheld.

A quest of noble gallantry
  sent forth the mighty ship.
And we, who watched her sailing
  wrung our hands and bit our lip.

For the land to which she voyaged,
  we knew had now decreed,
strength and might and power
  were all the virtues they would need.

And kindness, now, within this land
  was in such a low supply,
that the people scarce recalled it.
  They'd forgotten how to try.

For cruelty is contagious,
  selfish apathy is too.
And left unchecked, unchallenged,
  destroy much before they're through.

Yet still she travels patiently
  through darkness, storm and wind.
And us? We hold on fiercely
  to our hope that knows no end.

For we, who've seen her beauty
    can bear witness to the fact,
  that mighty walls have tumbled
    all because of one kind act!

Struggles

Wouldn't it be wonderful
  if struggles
were like snuggles.

Warm and fuzzy
  cuddly, cozy.
fun like blowing bubbles.

But struggles aren't
  that way you know,
they're vacuum-packaged troubles.

And when traveling in
  teams and pairs,
you'll think you're seeing double.

And sometimes problems
  breach the walls,
turning life to rubble.

But here's something
  to remember
when you step into life's puddles.

Even though some
  days are like
a thousand pieces puzzle.

You're made of something
  stronger, than even
great big muscles.

A holy strength
  to steady you
when knees begin to buckle.

So hang in there!
  And don't forget -
Kingdom growth is subtle.

Somedays Life Eludes Me

On somedays life eludes me
  because I fail to see
the beauty of creation
  on every side of me.

I rush, hurried, past the flower
  and notice not the bird,
and miss the tender singing,
  of choruses unheard.

For I'm a busy person
  and time is fleeting by,
and though I can't do everything
  I seem to want to try.

And so, blind, to so much beauty
  and deaf to nature's song,
I often live in ways, unwise,
  too frantic, manic, wrong.

But I think I'll choose another way
  today before I leave.
I think I'll pray for wisdom,
  for openness to receive.

For life, indeed is fleeting,
  and time, with hurried speed,
whispers to my wearied soul
  of a true and deeper need.

For joy is for the seeker,
  who stops to breathe and gaze,
who finds the art of simple things
  to brighten busy days.

Like ice cream cones and fishin' poles,
  fun on playground swings.
Let's you and I slow down a bit,
  and see what this day brings.

Ten Days Left

What if you only had ten days left,
  or maybe just five, or two?
Would you look at the world any differently?
  Tell me. Whaddya think you'd do?

Would you call your son or daughter,
  or maybe your mom or dad?
How 'bout that card you've been meaning to send,
  or your smile that could make a heart glad?

Would you let go of all the bitterness
  that's been festering in your soul?
Would you finally relinquish the allusion
  that you are always in control?

Would you stop and smell a flower,
  or watch some children play?
Would you visit with an old friend?
  Tell me what would you do, today?

Would you give an extra hug today?
  And listen with greater care?
Would you work to help the hurting?
  And maybe pray an extra prayer?

Life is lived in moments,
  until one day they're all spent.
And then somewhere along the way
  we'll wonder where they all went.

But, if you're reading these few words,
  here's good news that I bring.
You're still alive! You still have time!
  So live! Love! Dance and sing!

What if you only had ten days left,
  or maybe just five, or two?
Would you look at the world any differently?
  Tell me. Whaddya think you'd do?

Listening

Come, listen child to a word of truth
   spoke, oft, from far and near.
The virtue of a simple gift,
   the gift of friends who hear.

For often there are words to say
   wrapped soft in sorrow's tears.
And heavier grows the burden,
   without a friend who hears.

Listening is a sacred act,
   a gift to comfort fear.
And all that's really needed,
   is one kind enough to hear.

Anytime a listening friend
   on any day of the year,
speaks value by the simple act
   of working hard to hear,

we grow a little closer,
   and we bring a little cheer,
for nothing speaks love louder
   than a loving, listening ear.

Hello Discouragement

Hello discouragement,
  my old friend.

Seeing you reminds me
  of other times,
  other visits.

I don't lament
  your drop ins
  like I once did.

Not sure why…

I think maybe seeing you again
  refreshes my call
  my purpose,
  somehow.

I know that may sound funny
to others who don't know you as I do,
  who don't understand our
  unique friendship.

Seeing you again reminds me
   of those to whom I feel most sent.
The broken,
  fragmented,
  forgotten,
  fed up and afraid.

The walking,
  functioning,
  closeted
  discouraged.

The ones who wake unrested
  and repose heart-weary.
The ones who choke back hidden tears
  and are oh so gifted
  at hiding their hurts,

their wounds,
their scars
and fears.

Seeing you
  reminds me of them
  and of my call
  and my work.

 Seeing you, I see
    my brother and sister
    sojourning pilgrims.
  And I recognize
    our striking
    unmistakable
    undeniable
    family resemblance.

Seeing you reminds me
    just how very much
    I love them.

And I do so love them.

So,
thanks for stopping by.
I'm not sure I could do
this work without you.

Until next time…

The Armor of God *(Ephesians 6:10-20)*

Strap on the belt and breastplate,
  the shield, the helmet, sword.
Ready yourself for battle,
  you soldier of the Lord.

But not a violent posture
  against a human foe.
The battle now is fiercely waged
  'gainst hated, sin and woe.

Principalities have gathered
  from regions dark and stained.
Poised to bring destruction
  like storm clouds bring the rain.

"Take up the armor" says the word.
  "Put on the armor," true.
For the spiritual battle waging,
  requires more of you, than you.

But God doth never leave us
  to the limits of our might.
But places in our hand and heart
  the tools of truth and light.

So battle on beloved,
  stand for justice, goodness, grace.
For one day soon, we'll take the hill
  and weep to see his face.

The Silence Said

For contemplative types like me
  and maybe you, and you.
I often seek for answers
  for the things I wish I knew.

And often when I'm seeking,
  I'll speak a quite prayer.
And call to the God of silence,
  I trust is always there.

For I do not hear God speaking
  the way I hear your voice.
And o'er the years I've made my peace,
  call it faith, or choice.

'Cause listening to the quiet,
  stills my heart and mind.
Inviting me to deeper thought
  than words can help me find.

I've found in times of searching,
  oft times in deep distress
that silence holds a mystery
  the world does not possess.

So I keep bringing questions
  packed inside my head.
'Cause o'r the years I've learned to trust,
  just like the silence said.

The Little Things

In the course of human history
   mighty conquests
   or devastating defeats
   have often turned
   on something small,
   perceived insignificant
   at the time.

A word,
a phrase,
a gesture
that inflamed
or exacerbated
or elevated
or complicated
  things.

Or,

  A word,
  a phrase,
  a gesture
  that healed
  or encouraged
  or welcomed
  or reconciled
    people.

It's funny how
  little things
  can make
  such a big impact.

Marriages
  relationships,
  communities,
  churches,
  companies,
  families
  are built up

or torn down
by small things.
Acts of goodness,
 or acts of evil.
 Light that shines
  or darkness that invades.

So I've come today
 to deliver a message.
Today, you've been
 put in charge -
of the little things.

The Hope I Hold

I hold a hope deep in my soul,
   in soil that's dark and deep.
A hope that's not for sale or trade,
   a hope I long to keep.

This hope I hold I did not make,
   nor did achieve nor win.
It's something more akin to seed
   that's planted deep within.

And through this hope I see the world,
   it's broken fragments clear.
Reminding me in the darkest night,
   that dawn is drawing near.

I believe one day that this good hope
   will be beauty shared by all.
And on that bright and glorious day
   we'll shake the remnants of our fall.

This hope is not beholden
   to the struggles of our day,
nor is it weak nor wearied
   by the doubt, that doubters say.

It's hope that opens up my eyes
   to things I cannot see.
And I will not stop hoping
   for what I know will one day be.

So standing, I will stand today.
   Resolute, strong and bold.
Thanking God for this steadfast gift.
   God's gift - the hope I hold.

Sometimes I Laugh

Sometimes the world feels heavy,
  my shoulders strained,
  mind racing.
  Weary.

Sometimes I worry over
  things I can't control,
  or fix.

I can be discouraged
  sometimes.

Sometimes I'm tired,
  fatigued
  in body, mind
  and spirit.

Sometimes its difficult.
  Life.
  Sometimes life is just hard.

But then…..

Sometimes I laugh.
I just laugh
  out loud.

A funny moment
  dances across
  the TV screen.

"The Office"
  does that for me.

"Andy Griffith" too.
Sometimes "SNL,"
  though not as much
  as it used to.

Sometimes its
  something
  a friend says.
A joke,
  a story,
  a moment,
  unplanned,
  unscheduled.

And I just laugh.

And then I remember!

I remember something,
  something very, very
  important.
I remember
  I like laughing.
I like laughing a lot.

Years ago my youth group
  at Centenary UMC
  gave me a framed print of
  Jesus laughing.

They told me
  that it reminded them of me.
I think that's one of nicest things
  anyone's ever said to me.

I like to think of Jesus laughing!
I like to think of Jesus playing
  with the children.
  Tag.
  Hide-n-seek.
  Peep-eye.
  Peek-a-boo.
I like to think God has
  a really great,
  neat,
  cool
  sense of humor.

I think laughter is a gift,
  a rich and robust gift
  from the Almighty
  who I'm inclined to believe
  chuckles with us,
  for us,
  and at us!

Especially at us.

I think laughter is good
  for the soul
  and the heart
  and the mind.

So, basically
  here's what I've come to say.
Whatever the world
  brings your way
 may you laugh
  a hearty laugh -
   today!

I Wish

I wish I had a dollar
  for all my swings and misses,
for all the times that I've been blind
  to life's sweet hugs and kisses.

If I had but a nickel
  for all the times I've erred,
or lacked courageous, trusting faith
  when frightened, anxious, scared.

Then I might have a nest egg
  to serve in later years,
and numbered fewer heartaches,
  fewer restless nights and tears.

But something else I might have,
  if I'd more often got it right.
I might tend to think too highly,
  might think my light's too bright.

So I take my bag of bumblings,
  filled with stumblings and mistakes,
like piles of gathered autumn leaves,
  from years of worn-out rakes.

And set my face, with thankful heart
  and welcome this new day.
Grateful to God who knows me best
  and loves me, anyway.

A Modest Hope

I have a modest hope.
I've long since laid aside
  the hope for the grandiose
  treasures that filled my mind
  and captivating my dreams
  in the days of my youth.

I once hoped for achievements,
  monumental and great.
I hoped for accomplishments,
  the kind that the ambitious
  seek for themselves
  and despise in others.

Through the years
I have hoped for many things.
A tower-like life
  reaching to heaven.
Like the bounty of Babel
  boasting to make
  a name.
  My name.

There was a time,
  maybe not so long ago
  when securing status
  made sense,
  seemed sweet,
  and assured,
  and warranted,
  well-deserved.

I'm not sure when things changed.
Maybe one day I tasted status,
  and found it sweet,
  but not satisfying.

Perhaps I saw the folly,
  in myself and others,
  of pursuing,

chasing,
lusting
after temporal things,
fleeting accolades,
the momentary spotlight
and fading applause.

These days,
I have a modest hope.
I can't point you to the pivot,
   can't tell you when
   things changed.

Maybe one day
   I simply looked in the mirror
   and saw below the surface.
Could it be I simply saw
   beneath the pretense,
   underneath the facade,
   behind the persona,
into that prickly, dark
   and quiet place
   of hidden sin
   deftly tucked away
   from view.

Perhaps I saw myself,
   less confidant
   yet more clearly.
A sinner,
   sad and lowly,
   weak in the face of temptation,
   vulnerable,
   broken,
   undeserving
   of the slightest crumb
   that falls underneath
   the children's table.

And yet, beloved.

Beloved!

I'm not sure when
   or where or how
   I saw
   myself clearly.
Was it a Bible verse?
A song on the radio?
A smile from a stranger?
Did I see it in a tear of the aged,
   or hear it
   in the laughter of a child?

But somehow,
   seeing myself
   more clearly
became a window
   for me seeing me
   the way I became
   convinced that
God's sees me.

A perfect example
   of imperfection.
An under-whelming,
   under-performing
   under-achieving
   underling.

And yet, beloved.

Beloved!

So today,
I have a modest hope.

I simply want you to know
I've simply been sent
   to tell you -

that you're beloved too!

Dear Hope

Dear hope,
I've learned through the years
how essential you are
to the human spirit.
Intertwined,
and intermingled,
the unmistakable
fruit of faith.

Of course,
there are days
and weeks,
months
and seasons
when you seem
illusive,
distant,
fleeting,
hard to find.

Those are
difficult days
and weeks,
months
and seasons.

It's hard
without you
hope!

But one thing
I've learned about you
through the years
is the resiliency
of your nature,
and the unpredictability
of your appearing.

In the midst of the darkness
let the door crack
ever so slightly,
and a sliver of light
races across
the floor.
wreaking havoc
on the darkness.

In the slightest
uneven crack
of a hot, dry
sidewalk,
out of nowhere,
suddenly,
something
unmistakably green and
undeniably alive
breaks through.

Hope!
You are resourceful,
resilient,
relentless.
You are beautiful,
bountiful,
contagious,
winsome
and wonderful.

In the midst of
division and
discord,
disharmony and
disunion,
destruction
and despair
you find a way.

You appear
in simple ways.

An act of kindness,
a word of grace,
a gentle smile,
a patient ear,
an understanding nod,
a handshake,
a hug,
a card,
a call,
a tear.

Your fruit is
understanding,
respect,
forgiveness,
love,
goodness
and grace.

A light shines
and life breaks through
and we are changed
somehow.
We are transformed,
renewed,
reborn,
resurrected.

Hope!
Thank you for dropping by.

Please do come again!

Who Are You?

We've seen you sometimes,
   at work or at play,
seen work that you've done,
   heard words that you say.

Interactions you've had
   with stranger and friend
lead us all to believe
   your life's not a dead end.

But who are you really,
   deep down, underneath?
What are your worries,
   your goals and your dreams?

What gives your life meaning,
   what makes your heart tick?
What causes you anguish,
   what makes your soul sick?

Cause here's what I'm thinking,
   as I think about you.
I think you're worth knowing
   better than we oft do.

And others, as well
   if we took the time,
we could get to know better,
   the heart, soul and mind.

So maybe today,
   let's try, you and me
to look closer at others,
   trying harder to see.

Let's seek to find value
   believing its there.
And seeing, perhaps
   we'll give greater care.

Perhaps seeing others
  like we wish to be seen
we could change the world slowly,
  turn nightmares to dreams.

We could grow in compassion,
  be more loving and kind.
Who are you really?
  That's what's on my mind.

Consider This

A poet swims in water's deep
in search of dreams in gentle sleep.
And somewhere in that land unseen
imagination dreams a dream.

And in the moment when the pen
discovers where the road begins,
some deeper truths, unearthed are found
and dreams at once are freed, unbound.

The preacher, meanwhile crafts her craft
in ocean vast, on tiny raft.
And praying, searching for the word
that somehow helps God's truth be heard.

And teacher, with clear lesson plan
longs to help us understand,
that we might somehow grow to be
like strong and fruitful olive trees.

Musicians play a haunting tune
that makes the weary heart to swoon.
And we recall some simpler times
with ice cream cones and nursery rhymes.

Consider this, I heard him say
just before the break of day.
Dreams are not just fruit of night
but flourish well in brightest light.

So poet, preacher, musician, teacher
or whatever - you creative creature,
don't hesitate to dream your dream
for live's not always what it seems.

And help us see life's joys we miss,
like laughter, song, a gentle kiss.
So let us live with joyful heart.
And today, this day, is where we start!

That Other Road

I didn't have to be who, or what, I am.
I could have been something, or someone, different.

The road I chose long ago set me
   in the direction that's brought me here.

I didn't chose this road in isolation, though.
I've had help. A lot of help.

God, for one. Let's start there.
But there were other influences.

Other people helped me chose this road.
I liked the people I saw, and met, on this road.

Over the years, I've enjoyed their company.
Traveling with them, somehow made me want to be better.

My fellow travelers have inspired me, nurtured me,
   helped me stay on this road.

Of course it didn't have to be that way.

I easily could have made a different choice.
I could have chosen that other road.

I could have given into my baser self,
   could have wallowed in my inner darkness.

I could have cultivated bitterness, prejudice and pride.
I could have fed the anger and hatred within.

I could have chosen lust over love,
   violence over peace, judgment over grace.

There was some appeal, I must admit.
I saw some pretty cool people on that other road.

I saw people who had things I thought I wanted,
   power, success, relevance.

I didn't have to be who, or what, I am.
I could have been something, or someone, different.

I think of that truth, sometimes.
I think of all the good influences I've had.

I think of all the good people who have shaped me,
   formed me, accepted, welcomed and loved me.

And I realize not everyone is as fortunate as me.

Still, I'm not always what I should be, or can be, or desire to be.
I'm never quite worthy of the love, grace and goodness of God.

But every now and then I'm reminded that any goodness
   coming from me never begins with me.

I'm acutely aware that I didn't choose this road on my own.
Left to my own devices, I may have chosen that other road.

But I didn't, thanks to the influence of the goodness of others.
   I'm grateful for all who've helped me choose this road.

I'm grateful for all those fellow travelers who've chosen goodness,
   and who've helped me want to choose goodness, too.

I'm grateful that I've chosen this road.
I'm grateful I didn't chose that other road.

But, please dear God, let me never forget
  that in any moment, on any given day -

I still can!

My List of Overlooked Things

I dreamed I went to heaven,
   it seemed so real and bright.
The sky was clear as crystal,
   and it was never night.

Then someone close beside me
   placed within my hand
a parchment filled with writing,
   and said I'd understand.

I read the title at the top -
   "My list of overlooked things."
And I read the list for hours on end,
   at least, that's how it seemed.

The list was filled with beauty,
   with things alive with grace.
Things like children laughing,
   and a kindly neighbor's face.

And as I read my life flashed by,
   a new thought crossed my mind,
that if I had another chance
   I wouldn't be so blind.

I'd find a way to listen more,
   I'd look with softer eyes.
Attending to the beauty
   I'd so often hurried by.

Just then I woke, with quite a start
   and rubbed each sleepy eye.
And grateful it had been a dream,
   I resolved this day to try.

I'd try to see the overlooked,
   unnoticed, seldom seen.
The smiles, the joy and beauty
   I'd remembered in my dream.

My list of overlooked things
   was far too long for me.
O God, please give me ears to hear,
   and please Lord, eyes to see.

When Words Become Weapons

When words become weapons
  our baser selves win.
When our words pierce and maim
  we are steeped in hell's sin.

And when they are used
  as red meat for the crowd,
the weaponized words
  make our sin clear and loud.

When the words that we use
  are dug from hell's dirt
they divide and destroy,
  demean, break and hurt.

And here's what I know
  to be painfully true.
I know words that can kill,
  and I bet you do too.

But I know other words
  filled with beauty and grace,
that can build up and value
  every nation and race.

So here's my strong hope
  as I enter this day.
Let my words build a world
  that's more Christ-like, today.

If I Had One Prayer to Pray

I tend to pray a good bit.
Each morning.
Every night.
Occasionally through the day.
At meals,
during corporate worship,
at church events,
often at meetings,
in counseling sessions
and pastoral visits,
sometimes at Rotary.

Mostly extemporaneously,
but sometimes I pray
prayers written by others,
like the Psalms
or church fathers
or Christian leaders.

Sometimes my prayers are thoughtful,
rising deep from my soul,
at other times my prayers are
surface and shallow.

But what if I had only one prayer to pray?
One final prayer,
one last offering,
one final word,
one last petition,
one final song of praise,
one last prayer.

If I only had one prayer to pray,
I would hope it would focus
more on God than my self-interest.
I would hope that it would be a prayer
of authentic praise and adoration.

I would want my one prayer
to speak a word of grace and hope
for a fallen, broken, bruised and battered world.

Dear God let my one prayer
be a prayer for the other,
the outcast, ostracized, pushed away,
for the excluded and cast-out,
for the vulnerable, the weakest,
for the poor and downtrodden,
for the stranger, the refugee,
for the hurting and oppressed.

Lord let my prayer,
my one prayer,
be a prayer of welcome
and hospitality.

A prayer of understanding,
and inclusion
and sensitivity
and compassion.

In other words,
may my one prayer
honor Christ
and be consistent with your nature.

If I had one prayer to pray,
dear God in heaven,
I hope and pray that
there would not be
even the slightest remnant of me -
only Jesus.

The Gift

A man once traveled through our town,
  his gait was slow and steady.
I didn't notice him at first,
  perhaps I wasn't ready.

But when I finally noticed him,
  curiosity began to grow.
I wasn't sure what interested me,
  but somehow, had to know.

So I stopped the man one day in town
  and asked him for his name.
And many other questions too,
  like how, and why, he came.

But the answers seemed mysterious
  from the man who'd come to town.
And it seemed no matter how I tried,
  I couldn't pin him down.

And finally after some time spent
  he gently took my hand.
And pressing firm inside my palm
  said, "one day you'll understand."

"But what's it called" I pleaded,
  for I saw not one thing there.
"It's called a poem" he whispered
  and vanished in thin air.

Oft I've thought throughout the years
  of that gift placed in my hand.
I've long-since learned his words were true,
  for now I understand.

For the poet guides to deeper truths
  than I could find myself,
reminding me of memories
  hidden on some dusty shelf.

And the poet helps me see things
   like beauty, life and pain,
in ways that help me find some sun
   in days of storm and rain.

So I'm grateful for the simple gift
   placed in my hand that day,
and for the poet who speaks for me
   when I have no words to say.

Things I've Learned from Children

I've learned a few things in my day
  from the very wise and learned,
things that've served me well through time
  enriching my discerning.

Professors, teachers, scholars, authors
  have filled and stirred my mind,
and helped to grow a hunger
  within, for learning over time.

But many things I've learned in life
  far from a class room setting,
like laughter, joy and wonder
  I'm often prone to forgetting.

From children I have learned to see
  in ways the years had blinded,
opening my eyes to truths
  long forgotten, now reminded.

A flower springing from the earth
  a leaf once green, now red,
and story fairies dancing
  in tales, soft told, 'fore bed.

And greater truths, and noble
  like trust and faith and hope,
helping weary hands hold fast
  at the end of life's frayed rope.

And so today, among the prayers
  perhaps you and I can pray,
will be for children everywhere
  to know God's love today.

For children teach in child-like ways
  lessons we're wise to learn.
And every child deserves to know
  they're valued in return.

So thank you God, for children
　who hold our hands today
and lead us to your kingdom,
　skipping along the way.

When You Don't Know What to Do

Life can be a challenge,
  my friend you know its true.
And the challenge just increases
  when you don't know what to do.

Considering a purchase
  of car, or house, or shoes.
And though you weigh the pros and cons
  still, you don't know what to do.

A family gathers 'round the bed,
  as death is drawing near,
trying to make decisions
  steeped in grief, confusion, fear.

Life changes in a moment
  for a spouse who never thought
that life would act so cruelly,
  turning long-held plans to naught.

Divorce was never in her plan,
  now she's a single mom.
She strains to see the road ahead
  enveloped in the fog.

Uncertainty is crippling
  when confidence is weak.
And we just can't find the words to say
  when there are no words to speak.

So friend, I've simply come to say
  that I care and understand,
and that if you keep on reaching
  you may yet find a hand.

And here's a truth to hold inside
  your heart before you're through,
that may offer you some solace
  when you don't know what to do.

The best that we can hope for
   on even given day
is to do the best we know to do,
   say the best we know to say.

And if God wills to bless us
   with an extra drop of grace,
we may just find our best today
   is enough for this day's race.

So take the risk beloved,
   though you don't know what to do.
'Cause with God's grace, and with your best,
   I'm putting all my chips on you!

God of the Insignificant

What determines the value of a life?
Who gets to decide?
How is a human life measured,
what scales are used?

Is human life measured in inches,
or by possessions,
or accomplishments,
or accolades,
or wisdom
or education?

Who are the insignificant of the world?
Who are the obsolete,
the discarded,
the unimportant
and rejected,
the broken,
battered
and abused?

How does God feel
about the insignificant of the world?

Where is God?

God is hidden
among those counted least
by worldly measure.
The poor,
the old,
the sick,
the foreigner,
the vulnerable and weak.

As it was in the foolishness of the cross,
so it remains.
God still topples human wisdom,
scoffs at human power,
hiding his face
from the haughty,
arrogant and proud.

Jesus lived and died
in solidarity
with the depths
of human suffering.
To see him today
is to be yoked
to the hurting
and humiliated,
the abused
and hated,
the cast-off,
cast-out
and thrown away.

For who the world
sees as insignificant,
the Lord does not.

To learn this truth
is to travel a rough
and dangerous road
that leads to death,
a death from which
life springs forth.

And this road has a name -

the way of the cross.

A Friend I Found

A friend I found the other day,
  it was not in my plan.
I was not really searching,
  perhaps you understand.

A conversation started,
  and then before I knew
I found the joy of being heard
  before our talk was through.

A smile, a nod, a gesture,
  with understanding eye,
energized my spirit
  and gave my soul a sigh.

A friend I found the other day
  with patient, listening ear,
and left our brief chat grateful
  for times when friends draw near.

Friends come to us in many ways,
  some briefly, some for life.
They make the journey easier,
  and help us with the strife.

The friend I found the other day
  reminded me again, that
of all the ways I'm known, I hope
  I'm truly known, as friend.

I Stand With You

For every broken hearted traveler,
  every wounded soul,
for the forgotten,
  the excluded,
  marginalized,
  pushed away,
  knocked down,
  discarded,
  demeaned,
  disrespected,
  demoralized and
  diminished,
I stand with you.

For every one who grieves,
   all who grope in the fog,
for everyone who is lost,
   afraid,
    forgotten,
    invisible,
I stand with you.

For the oppressed,
   the mistreated,
   the ill-used,
for all who are beaten,
   battered
   and bruised
by cruel words
   and hate-filled speech,
   by bigotry,
   prejudice
   and racism,
for all who are judged
   and treated unjustly,
   victimized
by every dehumanizing
   behavior
   born of hell,
and unworthy of Christ,
I stand with you.

Life is a journey of becoming,
   an ongoing discernment
   of who we will be,
   and who we will follow,
   and where we will stand.

Lord Jesus,
   through your suffering
   death on the cross
   you stand in solitary
   with all who suffer.

Dear Christ,
   friend of the hurting,
   the weak,
   the vulnerable
   and oppressed,

I stand with you.

Give Yourself a Break!

Sometimes life is hard, confusing,
and since Monday's a good day for musing,
this advice, don't be refusing
especially if your mirror's accusing.

Give yourself a break!

No I mean it, I'm really quite sincere,
and hopeful that you'll lend an ear
to a truth worth speaking far and near,
especially in times of anxious fear.

Give yourself a break!

Cut yourself some slack,
it's not because you lack the knack,
it's just hard when its hard and that's a fact,
and besides, beloved, we've got your back!

Give yourself a break!

Extend yourself some grace,
put a smile on that cool face,
sneaker up, and join the race,
even if you don't win, or place.

Give yourself a break!

Cause here's something you should know,
in times of sun and rain and snow,
your halo still has plenty of glow,
there's still pep in your step, good get up and go.

So….

Give yourself a break!

Okay, so you don't have all the answers,
neither did the June Taylor Dancers,
nor all those Hollywood romancers,
or charging cavalries with sharpened lancers.

Give yourself a dad-gum break!

So get out there and do your best,
and trust the good Lord for the rest,
'cause believing in you is not a jest,
for you're a blessing, 'cause you're blessed!

Give yourself a break!

O Simon Peter, I Understand

The rebuke must've felt sharp.
Coming, as it did, so quickly.
Cutting, as it did, so deeply.
The trouble was with your mind,
or to be more precise,
where you had set it,
on human things
not on divine things.

O Simon Peter, I understand.

I set my mind on human things, too.
I set my mind on human things,
lesser things,
temporal things,
fading away things.
I set my mind
on turning to dust
and rust
and decaying things.

I set my mind on me –
longing for what eludes me
growing impatient about things not to my liking,
lamenting my limitations.

Like you, Simon Peter, I set my sights too low.
Like you, Simon Peter
I need to hear again
that my hope does not rest in me
or even in those dear to me.
My ingenuity, my strengths,
my talents, my abilities,
on my very best day
will always fall far short of the bar.

My station
my status
my striving
does not,
will not satisfy.

Jesus, like Simon Peter
I deserve your swift rebuke
I am exposed,
convicted by your
stern and saddened stare.
Like Simon Peter
I keep getting it wrong,
keep missing the mark,
keep messing up.

Yet, even with the rebuke
ringing in his ears
you allowed him to follow you,
bidding him
and me
and all who would follow
to deny ourselves
take up our cross
and follow you.

And so he did,
and so I must,
and so we will.

O Simon Peter, I understand.

Accepted

Life is not always easy.
And sometimes it's
  really not
always easy.

Some seasons
  are filled with
  stress,
  remorse,
  guilt,
  grief,
  regret,
  sadness,
  shame,
  and heartache.

Sometimes, if we're not careful
  we can give into the
  dark voices that
  troll our souls.

The voices that tell us
  tainted truths
  about ourselves.
Voices that whisper lies,
  "You're no good!"
  "You're a failure!"
  "You're unlovable!"
  "You're unredeemable!"

Just incase
    it's one of those seasons,
    and the wolves are
    at your door,
    and the inner voices
    are piercing,
    and relentless,
    and life-draining,
I have come to bring you
    another word

that describes you,
a word truer than
the words whispered
 from the shadows,
 or the sidelines.

Accepted!

You are accepted
 just as you are,
 with all your imperfections,
 your penchant
 for mistakes,
 missteps
 and blunders.

Accepted!

You belong!
You matter!
You are beloved,
 valued,
 cherished,
 unique.
Accepted!

You are accepted.
 Without condition,
 prerequisite
 or requirement.

Accepted!

Created in the image of God.
 Redeemed by Christ,
 renewed in love,
 restored by grace.

Accepted!

You are accepted!

The Lesson of the Sea Squirt

Listen child, lean closer,
  hear my cautionary tale.
About the little sea squirt
  who frolics in sea's shell.

Learned scientist tell us
  that curiously they roam,
exploring ocean's bottom,
  their first and forever home.

Inching toward a food source,
  scurrying away from harm,
a constant life of movement,
  unfazed by calm, or storm.

Until one day the sea squirt
  tires beneath the sea,
no more scurrying to or fro,
  no desire to be free.

And so the weary sea squirt
  affixing to rock or boat,
finds a permanent place to be,
  ceasing its curious float.

And before it's story's over,
  our little watery friend
makes a meal out of its own brain
  'fore life comes to an end.

Perhaps there is a lesson
  in the sea squirt's sorted tale,
that curious minds are good things
  and moving serves us well.

So read a book, recite a poem,
  stay curious every day.
Keep learning, thinking, growing
  and don't forget to play!

Ode to My Worry Wart

I have a little worry wart
  who lives inside my head,
often stopping by for coffee,
  or following me to bed.

And oft' my little worry wart
  has many thoughts to share.
With many wart-like whispers
  'bout trouble, fear, despair.

And if I am not careful
  my worry wart takes charge,
making even little hills
  seem mountainously large.

It's then my mind grows frantic
  and hand-wringing ensues.
And it's hard to hear the birds sing
  o'er my worry wart's sad blues.

But sometimes in the fever
  an uncommon quiet soars,
though gentle as a butterfly,
  like great Aslan it roars.

Reminding me of truer truths
  my soul needs to reclaim,
when storms and doubt assail me,
  mocking me by name.

That perfect love is given
  by One whose name is love,
who has the power to cast out fear
  like a Spirit-wafting dove.

And when my mind is clearer
  to truths, held fast and strong,
packing my worry wart's tiny bags,
  I wave and say "so long!"

The Visitor

It happened one night
many years ago.
I still remember like
it was yesterday.

Once, during a time
of great fear,
anxiety and uncertainty
in my life,
I heard a knock at my door.
It was a gentle knock.
It wasn't heavy handed,
intrusive
or demanding.

I opened the door.

At my invitation,
a visitor smiled
and entered.
Then, seated at my table
spoke softly -

"Take a breath,"
said the visitor.

"Breathe.

"You're weary,
tired,
anxious,
on edge.

"I know.

"Take a breath.

"Close your eyes.
Open your heart.
Trust.

Remember.
Breathe.
Believe.

"Believe
that all will be well,
that the broken will be made whole,
that the fragments will be gathered.
Believe that the light will shine
and hope will sing
and beauty will dance.

"Believe,"
said the visitor.

"Believe that
grace will reign,
that mercy
and compassion
are not in short supply.
Believe that love
will conquer,
that love will win.
Believe
that all will be well."

After these words
we sat in silence
for what seemed like hours.

Then standing to leave,
the visitor turned,
smiled, and said,
"Remember me.
Hold fast to me,"
and walked toward the door.

"Who are you?"
I asked, as the visitor
disappeared into the night.

"I am your faith,"
said the visitor.

"Remember me.
Hold fast to me."

And to this day,
whenever I'm afraid
or anxious
in the midst of
uncertain times,
I remember that night.
I remember that visit.
I remember the visitor.

And I find that
I always find comfort,
solace and strength
when I remember,
and hold fast….

…..to my faith.

I Am Lazarus

Entombed in the
dark and damp
cold clay of sin and death.

I'm not the biblical Lazarus.
I'm not a character
in John's story of Jesus.

But I am Lazarus.

At one time or another,
I've been where John
says Lazarus was.

Dead.
Buried.
Without light
or hope or life.

Entombed.
Defeated.
Breathless.

I've known the
shame of sin
and the weight of regret.
I've known the
allure of lust.
I've been seduced by
the sirens of pride
and greed
and prejudice.

I am Lazarus.

Beyond hope,
steeped in despair,
alone,
lifeless,
entombed.

Are you Lazarus too?

And yet I believe
in the voice that calls
my name from the
mouth of the tomb.

I believe in the One
who speaks my name,
the One who refuses
to give up on me,
the One who commands
the stone be rolled away,
undeterred by my stench.

I believe that the One
who spoke creation
into existence,
speaks my name.

I believe in the One
who commands
the diseases of
death and sin and despair
to unbind me and let me go.

I am Lazarus.

Are you Lazarus too?

It Wouldn't Matter Much

It wouldn't matter much,
   what I do or say,
if people were just objects
   who oft' get in my way.

And if I didn't see them
   the way a good heart should,
then it wouldn't really matter
   if I didn't seek their good.

If I saw the world as just my stage,
   with me in the starring role,
with cast and crew supporting
   and under my control.

Then I might just be guilty
   of placing myself too high,
overselling my importance
   with my head up in the sky.

It wouldn't matter much,
   should I choose this path,
if I criticized my neighbor
   or laughed behind his back.

But it seems this kind of life
   might be lonely in the end.
And it might just be a challenge
   to find, or keep, a friend.

And if I choose to live like this,
   aloof, beyond love's touch.
When I lay me down to die,
   it wouldn't matter much.

I Didn't Think I'd Die Today

I didn't think I'd die today,
  I had so much to do.
So many tasks before me,
  miles from being through.

Unfinished tasks, unmet goals,
  files stuffed full with plans.
And so I labored on as if
  I did not understand

that the frailty of life absorbs
  the life I call my own.
So I plunged ahead, forgetting
  that my life is just on loan.

I didn't think I'd die today,
  so I didn't realize,
and failed to even notice
  my very last sunrise.

And conversations that I took
  for granted 'oft before,
now seem to me more sacred,
  passing through the spectral door.

The amends that I considered
  making long before the end,
give me some regret just now.
  I will not try and pretend.

And the cards I meant to write,
  like the words I meant to say,
may not haunt me for eternity
  but sure make me sad, today.

I didn't think I'd die today.
  But I guess it goes to show,
that life is far more fleeting
  than the living ever know.

CPSIA information can be obtained
at www.ICGtesting.com
Printed in the USA
BVHW052047310123
657555BV00010B/53